THE COMPOSITION OF GLASS

PHILLIP FOSS

THE COMPOSITION OF GLASS

———————————

Lost Roads Publishers
Number 34   Providence 1988

ACKNOWLEDGEMENTS:

Thanks to the National Endowment for the Arts for a fellowship in poetry which made completion of this work possible.

Some of these poems have appeared in *Conjunctions, Hambone, Notus, Southpaw,* and *Temblor* whose editors we thank for permission to reprint.

Foss, Phillip.
                    The composition of glass / Phillip Foss
                        P.   CM. ——— (Lost Roads ;   No. 34)
              ISBN 0-918786-38-X   (pbk.) : $7.95
              I. Title.
      PS 3556.0755C6   1988
      811'.54———dc19   88-17021
                                                                 CIP

CONTENTS

For Joyce

THE FUGITIVE MUSIC

THE FLOWER EMERGED FROM HER THROAT

The bodies were lain neatly along the road. They were either humans or warnings or birds. This was the premise around which life was structured, in the same way that the grounds around a pavilion are landscaped to lessen the shock from wilderness to etiquette.

It made no difference that the bodies were on another continent, or decomposed, since it seemed that their weight contributed to the world's rotation, like handles which the moon pulled and illuminated, thus making their expressions, or skulls, apparent to those, possibly in love, who happened to walk by.

That the bodies existed only in memory was trivial since everything, at least of importance, existed only in memory. Recall the pavilion's stone walls carved with poems, from memory, or the lovers who seek to forget everything.

The bodies are beside a river and there are also bodies in the river. These do not become mirrors of those on land, nor does the river mirror the stars or the moon which pulls. Neither are they like white fish floating since the water around them makes the water within them disintegrate.

There are no bodies in the air, only the common breeze with its odors of the living: smoke, incense, fruit. And the odor of dead things, like words and summer and caress.

None of these are intended as portraits other than that they were flowers which opened and closed with the light or the season.

THE ESSENTIAL QUALITY OF EXISTENCE IS THE DISPLACEMENT OF SPACE

This is redundant,
a clock interminably sounding six,
that is, the season with its peculiar opulence and work,
so redolent in its charm that the petty wildflowers
seem opaque, in the way a person's eyes appear
when they are thinking other than they are speaking,
for instance commenting on lack of appearance
or weather with the obligatory eyebrows
and hands in motion like strange small animals
trying to disengage themselves from a larger beast,
or just as often some redundant remark
about the season and its opulence
as if it were enough to merely observe
and not participate in all that ending,
like being able to anticipate the last drop
in a rain storm or any other contrived
finalé with or without curtain or bow
or character or the subject or idea
beyond the mere appearance of formality
and regularity, like a clock interminably sounding six,
or a woman whose lips have disengaged themselves
from her face, as from a larger beast,
and continue their recitation which is not
about love or food, but of a grander vision
of the world, something like truth, wherein
everything will be revealed and resolved,
thus becoming boring and dead,
the silence at the end of a recording,
a lost garment mistaken for a body,
the apparent density of darkness inside water,

or the way the odor of carrion
forms a grander invisible body unsusceptible to wind,
and all other images appropriate to describe
the unremarkable or unspeakable,
wherein, perhaps, a whole other version exists,
or is possible, including stars and a sea-side walk
with music, or, if not, sea birds,
or perhaps another with an old man and fire and coffee
and the odor of pipe smoke, not death, but the coziness
of night, all of which leads to the realization
of possibility and failure, like an opera singer
practicing the sounding of noise over and over and over
deluded by what hope to resolve what pain.

NOT LIKING THE SOUND, YOU COMMIT YOURSELF
TO ANONYMITY

Because the dream was exquisitely fabricated from plywood
you chose the green of the actual tree as a point of departure.

*

The distance you have to travel is reduced to the sound which
appears to have the texture of a tortoise shell, yet to be
red like lipstick.

*

This distinctiveness makes it easy for your mind to wander
back to its disorientation, a state you conclude is due to
meteor showers and the unusual odor of the rains.

*

You recall that their voices did not fit their bodies, as if
they were lipping a recording, thus giving them the appearance
of sitting very distantly, their voices reaching you lapsed.

*

Beside being ugly, what they said was cliché, though striking
you as revelatory, like noticing the landscape and realizing
that you are somewhere other than you had assumed.

*

All of this, of course, contributes to your paranoia about
yourself, a state requiring constant vigil even in sleep,
due to the unnatural momentums of which you are capable,
such as impulsively killing the dog, or laughing.

*

Because the meteor showers and the rains occurred simultaneously,
you became resistant to the concept of gravity and hurled
objects to the floor in an attempt to preceed it, like suicide.

*

But this seemed cliché, like their faces, which were red
and green, the lips and eyes, yet seemed revelatory, like
mistaking someone in a crowd for someone dead.

*

This, of course, contributes to your fear of crowds and
the manner in which people adjust their bodies in response
to gravity, the way a dog's body is seduced, or consumed.

*

That the whole dream was exquisitely fabricated from plywood
you interpret as meaning that it was like a tortoise shell,
not in terms of defense, but designed as a container wherein
individuals could sit and speak.

*

Yet you have a problem meshing with the rhythm of that speech,
like being unable to skate to music, to posture your body
correctly in relation to the ice and gravity, which makes
you fall slightly too slow, the sound of your body striking
lapsed.

*

This accentuates your disorientation, making you afraid you
will wake doing something other than sleeping, impulsively
laughing or seeking an actual tree as a point of departure.

*

But the trees are anonymous, or at least sufficiently regimented,
to preclude finding one, thus leaving you disoriented in regards
to direction, other than down.

*

You decide on naming, as both a method and recreation and invent
a vocabulary which precludes communication, the way you can
wake into a room exquisitely fabricated of plywood.

*

Yet disliking the sound of the language you abandon it,
giving preference to mere tangibility and its attendant
anonymity.

*

Unlike a description of the odor of rain, your assurances
come too late for placation or satisfaction, given their
textures and your failure to make correct distinctions.

*

So your manner of thinking and its relationship to the rain,
both of which you are suspicious and tired, prevent you.

CONFUSING GREEN WITH THE COLOR RED: ALLEGORIES

In the rearview mirror the truck following him was going backward.

The body in the ditch was not dead, only crazy.

Though walking, the ladies fat.

After his irises turned white he craved marrow.

The twisting smoke was birds.

Watching dead people on television.

Though having forgotten he remembered there was some reason for this.

Listening to dead people sing on the radio.

The purple cactus, after his head was damaged.

Hating the way the old lady sat.

Although crazy, he seemed to walk all right.

Why is it going to be tomorrow.

Given the opportunity to be a fool he hoped to kill them.

When the car flipped its hood yawned.

Confused because the deep cut failed to bleed.

Although not drunk, his mind like sideways.

If he left there would be nowhere right to go.

Neat triangles of glass embedded in his forehead

Irrigating the corn the water was full of large fish.

It was amusing the way the ocean tried to kill him.

Because the one character became crazy he became.

His eyes were fishy, like a fish bowl.

It was probably hereditary that his hands would not come off.

The woman was carrying the dead monkey by its tail.

He believed the river was a calendar.

In the rock carving the woman had amateur genitals.

It sounded like wind rattling tin, his truck crushing him.

He had forgotten that he always saw his face backward.

They took the offal home in a wheelbarrow.

Her mother having drowned in the bathtub she took swimming lessons.

The roof of its mouth was black naturally.

The dead man kept his hand held up for two hours.

Either he or the room was shaking.

The corpse was dehydrated so it fit in the drawer.

Because it was often cold he dreaded the snow.

He couldn't drop the cat because it had bitten through his thumb.

They ate all the puppies.

Why when he shut his eyes her lips were green.

When he awoke his fears were in the room.

After staring at him for a while it was obvious his eyes were upside down.

Stabbing its stomach the gas was released.

They were pitchforking fish onto the bank.

Although blind he would look at you.

The music tried to make him faint.

He couldn't understand the deaf man's writing.

Though he could barely walk her ankles seemed erotic.

At his birthday party they killed him.

He couldn't understand why it was called nonsense.

It made animal sounds, his boot full of blood.

Finally he knew he knew nothing.

You look like a ghost, he said, after shooting himself through the head.

———

THE BACK OF HER NECK APPEARED TO BE A HAND WITH THE FINGERS EXTENDED

The clouds have
of clarity. Dissatisfaction in
those who smile. Has no
displacement
Her eyes as if
frame alludes to obliqueness. Smiling.
ravens kissing. The gray
ecast of rain. The cast
the temporal qualities
hill appears
grow with time. Always
neck. The absence
head speaking to him in
abstraction of image.

triangulated. The abuses
the politeness of
value beyond the
of space: him.
smiling. The bent
Two
cat possibly dead? The for
of the head. Reassessing
of space: the
to
a false epistemology, her
of silence: his
words: the

Beyond the fact of his embarrassment there was no discernable quality to his existence.

Believing himself to be alone, he lifted the stone gingerly, faithful that beneath it was a hole which could lead him to the center of the earth.

He asked when
tomorrow. The
blue to
radiance, the nature of placement
So long,
Beyond the dis-

it would be
relationship of
white, in terms of
in space.
it takes.
placement in space,

there was no dis-
his existence. The clouds seem
some arbitrary perimeter. God
above the clouds. Shoveling
The time it takes
with its water content. Why
stars during the day. About
she could be. A second
it takes
end of the house to the other.

cernable quality to
to define
is somewhere
dirt on the rooster.
to burn has to do
you cannot see
the robbery, morose
gone only. The time
to walk from one

And observed that there was no hole, nor was the earth of any different color, nor was there any creature which could be taken as a sign or symbol or hint at any meaning beyond the fact of lifting the stone as an act of, perhaps, faith, or superstition, or stupidity, yet more likely failure to accept.

The embarrassment if anyone had been watching.

Tomorrow we will be
accomplished today.
shell stuck to its chest.
was white. She found the white
beach. The sand was blue. The time
to walk to
to grow larger with time
consumed. It was a consuming
will, of course, experience settlement.

content with what we have
The bird has a blue egg
Its chest
shell on the
it takes
the island. Appears
and the distance
passion. You

It was a false way of looking at the world that prevented him from understanding that the rock itself was the center of the world.

To have known he was observed by the narrator would have been an embarrassment.

God watches over you. Why   the clouds
obstruct. When tomorrow   becomes clear. If it is
beyond the count   of your
fingers it is   many.

Yet there were stones everywhere

They were blue clouds and the sky was white.

Apparently her hair was white and her eyes blue.

Beyond its appearance as   a hand there
was no discernable quality to   her neck. That her neck
displaced space   as a neck
or hand was sufficient   reason for her
existence, tomorrow.

———————————

BECAUSE GIVING HIM AWAY HIS EYES

His cruel habits made it impossible
          for him to perceive that the world
had aged while he was unconscious.

          When the sun came back out
it was a different season,
                    one that lacked the lustre
of that which had preceeded it.

          The night was never an angel
but a bitter cage like his mouth,
                    its language incoherent.

And the fact that he could perceive
                    where a snake had passed
through the yard was distorting
          his ability to stand like a person.
He felt the weight shift within his body
                    like that of a shot-filled doll.

What was formal and thus disconcerting
          was the sky's texture and its relative
immobility in relation to his position
                              beneath it.

He recalled that there were several
                    words to approximate this
but could remember none.

That he was already dead seemed apparent
if not by his posture then by his eyes,
          which continued to be deceptive
in their laughter.

Because of this it was difficult
to communicate with humor and reason,
            as was required to maintain
his position in the appropriate
                        rooms and eyes.

But his religious aspirations
            had been usurped by a kind
of nostalgia; the same
    that causes a dead animal to collapse
into its shadow.

                He perceived this
and also perceived sunflowers
                    through the window,
which because of his eyes were yellow.

They questioned him regarding the amount
of darkness he had consumed.

                It was apparently the fire
in the house that had revealed
                        this appetite,
because of its sudden
                unjustified expression.

The trees were dead,
                but this was expected
due to the position they occupied
                in relation to his window:
he could touch the mountain
            without moving, his explanation,
though the intent was unintentional.

He could recognize none,
due to his eyes,
but knew their names
by their voices and thus felt
comfort and terror,
like lending your posture.

Their consensus was that the stones
about his house must be moved.
He accepted this as correct
due to his eyes
which had made him assume
they were stones.

Concerning his family
he was reticent, satisfied
in removal, something exquisite
like eclipse, he thought.

The problem revolved around
the notion of posture
which he couldn't explain, the way
dogs crouch before a sound.

Still, he was unable
to position himself correctly
in relation to the other
figures and considered
that by slapping his head
their positions might be altered
enough to move his eyes.

But their continued occupancy
forced him to retreat
in a unique manner

            so that his skin changed,
allowing him to blend
            with his clothing, he thought
his eyes, knew this,
            the way they winked,
when they looked at him,
            his eyes, their way.

Having found the way
            they were there
was no point in trying
            to change their bodies
or his
            position due to the angle
of the light
            which was depressed
through the window
            something like a bird
or the closure of eyelids.

            Perhaps he could remember
his life and the duration
            of that memory would meet
his death, thus moving
            him backward in some kind
of foolish display of ballet.

            But he knew from the eyes
of those watching him
            that his eyes
had betrayed him,
            and his posture
was deceptive through omission.

THE CHINESE POEMS: DISPLACEMENT

Granted   seasons   inappropriate   emotion   remains   displeasure   suicide
resistance   failure   perceive   life   clarity   manner   leaf
fall vertically   defiance   perceived force   individual   claustrophobia

manner she perceives   apparent passage   time   limiting   possibilities
world she interprets   her own   her control   realm   her emotional
need   perpetuates her identity   she   disturbed   repentant   resists
her face fall upward   sky

physical identity   blue   confused   emotional Isolation
intensified   confusion   objects   touch   sight   facets   face
projected   she   see everything   her   doubt

she   posit   life/face   redemptive   transcendent   grounded
promised land   prevents   eating   fruit   anticipation   greater

choice   watch   stars   anticipation   zodiac   animals
letters composing words   reading   salvation

DISPLACEMENT 2

He   rectified   memory   coincide   image   sees   tunnel descending   black
theater consumed   bodies   voices   dissonant odors   secondary image he
perceives: horses   slaughtered   black   white   projected memory colors   blood
red.   neither   symbols   womb   death   theater   image
    projection   memory

    question   perceive   train window leaving coincide
actual landscape passing   watching   film   ideal imagined landscape
        project out   window   create memory   later coddle

    problem: memory   include images   extend   conversation   movement
devoid   object   see   lights   city   moving picture   process
complete   speaking   odor   thought;   memory   own thought
time   prostitutes stood;   memory   taste   liquor   conversation
        foreign?

    distilled   whole world down   neat package   available
    recall   approximate   experiences   deletes   extraneous
painful   foolish   fashions   new world   selected pieces   memory
    leaves rest   die beyond   sea

ONEIRIC

Whether Dionysian or a metaphor for death he couldn't conclude regarding the vines sprouting as his eyebrows.

HAVING CONCEDED THAT HER LIFE WAS INAPPROPRIATE

The season fragile
    pines' posture interpreted as threatening
music debased into noise
    read the lines on her hand to reconstruct
if killing herself would be polite
        because the stream smelled of carrion
the bees were orange
  smoke hung an unlegged table in the room
constant vibration
                        the sea was marginal
romance misinterpreted as work
            the firewood seemed awkward
grass was aggressively sharp
            the shape of her lips unfamiliar
temptation to starve
                three strange men with rifles
confusion of the bed
                    floorboards overtly rotting
a lack of order in the sky
            the distance believed obscene
drugged quilt
    trepidation at the movement of windows
obvious silence around the lights
                persistent failure to dream
obsessed with the rigidity of shadow
                inference of displacement
having seen the bear
                    failure to articulate
finding time
        the placement of utensils on the tables
their shadows

                        confession of reluctance
a white horse in the road
                    chimney smoke redundant
the way of fingernails
                    her face resembling a horse
the black music
              anonymous fingerprints on the glass
debate the value of reincarnation
                            confusing the voices
collecting spiders
                      fearing the content of walls
if breathing someone else's breath
                  knew her interpretation was evil
if then appropriate

RESISTANCE TO PASSION

*A body at rest affords us no idea of any active power to move, and
when set in motion, it is rather a passion than an action in it.*
— Locke

Before, you could accelerate
a way of altering any landscape
with yucca or passion

                        without notation
                        be it embellished

with fragrance and the familiar
like flowers.

                    like a spring morning
                     voices dying off

with the degree of your desire,
and cause the cognition of things

                So, you equate the distance
                          or fear

wind-whipped and anonymous.

                     to flee past you,

the finer the pain;
to the way lightning

                Thus the higher the note
                   this is comparable
                     stains the eye.

Then night is the vehicle.

                    Nothing can move
yet the speed is crippling,   the way music is evil.

Being even, the flourishing
of attracting
                                        fades, a way

                         dissonance into the surge.

You remember the ecstasy
and has the texture of ice.
                         as a note which wavers

                         You would like to reinvent

that memory into something tangible,

                                     but you have lost
any sense of the placement   of experience
and thus it is elusive,   sliding about in your caricatures.

Perhaps that surge
the transformation of a body   was feminine,
                                            into sound.

The music then is not merely sexual,

                         but personified and the love
you feel is not displaced   passion,
but directed toward an object

                         not ephemeral, but living.

You have accelerated   into a negative momentum
and, like a bird   killed in flight, you continue
in the direction   of your desire,
even though its object no longer beckons or seduces

                                                        or exists.

What you see now   are only the relics
of your memory:

                                              a time trimmed

to an object, immobile, living.

                              Yet within your desire for reinvention
there is a futility   in your action,
like lifting a dead bird from the ground

                                      and spreading its wings

Now everything you have made and love   is scattered
behind you, alien   and distant,
seeming to bear the design

                              of other hands, or of no hands
but to merely be as they are, neither loved nor loving.

You are so dissatisfied   with your speed
that the notation which allows the music to enter

                                        is suspended.

Perhaps what is lacking   is concentration
or the passion

                                        to assimilate sound

as if it were food.

                                        In any case, you are coasting
possibly on water or sand,   and the friction
is less than you feared
                        but sufficient to produce a sound like an insect,
irritating, non-lyrical,
                                and you are dissatisfied that your voice
is hoarse,   making you mute
in embarrassment, and preventing you from overriding
                what is produced by sand or water by your own singing.

Having killed
must confirm

But there is only pessimism and confusion.
you

of lightning; a way of looking
If perpetual you concede there can be no closure.

is your ultimate fear and the attraction

Ending
the night is a flame.
the bodies are burned there

And finally you
walk out and count the fallen,
familial names

in excess you

its speed or lacking.
Instead
symbolize this as a forest

at night.

This

to killing.
is impossible through speech;
Even if

is the idea of incarnation.
must
granting them

and the appearance of devotion.

This is love:
stone as stasis,
implicit in the echo
off stone.
                                              assume the body as passion;
                                                             or the evil
                                                      of a bird's voice

                                              And the more evil the music,
the greater the speed.

                                            This is necessary for moving
the world;
                                            through which the hand can pass,
like a flesh,
                                                         a love.

Then what is sinister is movement:
                                                            No nothing.

It represents an aversion
                                                        to gravity
as the body in grace responds;
                                this is foretold by absolute ignorance
and is embraceable simply in defeat.

                                                We know nothing:
the passion of movement is without thought,
                                              the way the flames
from a burning house are exuberant, at dawn,
                                        adamant in destiny and nothing.

———————————

VIRGA. ICY GATE.

Progression proceeds
Define willow. The monastery
Sanctifying the wedding
Waters. Here there can be no thirst.
In the placement of pine
And the reflection is as convincing
Is reminiscent of something
To proceed in a manner
Yet progress cannot be measured
Of clouds,
Nor by the transition
To consider the human:
Or observer. The arrangement
Haphazard, the determinants
And the conclusion
Willow-river-cloud.

from conclusion. Baskets
beside the river is a god
of blue and brown
There is order
across the cliff
as the cliff
intangible. It is necessary
amenable to topography,
by the passage
or of their shadows across soil;
from red to gray. It is impossible
there is no language
of elements is deniably
inexplicable
invalid. Remaining:

There is no person; this is the liberating premise
and the conclusion: one step: one step: one step:
stone: dog: sea. Gravitation is the love all sought,
and the unifying dismay; the inevitable dread
of waking into matter, though all alternatives
mythically ruminate or are untenable annihilation.
To be without this burden of distance, to merely taste
unaware of the grand design; what separates?
What unseparates? Does the illusion begin?
Has begun? Will begin?:

                              There is a mingling of blue
and brown waters at the meeting of two streams
that represents the beginning of the river.
If you stand on the bank and observe this process
without prejudgement, it is interesting.

We have confused our redemption
And pain.
Our own geography, specificity:
Denied sleep; specificity:
We can no longer envelop ourselves
Heirlooms used to suppose duration.
Is beneficent, as always, lush.
Illusion which ends
Cradles what remains,
The meager screams with ostentation.
Will be forgotten by all,
Its light anywhere.
Pain is confused with red,

                    with several colors
          The purpose is to acknowledge
                        the obese land
                        green apples.
                      in the tattered
                           The light
              We proceed in a violent
         where nothing began. Redundancy
              specificity: crested wheat.
                       The afternoon
                    never laying bare
      The specificity will be in absence.
                    darkness with black.

A vocabulary of violence redeems itself

by being spoken in the presence of pain or darkness.

Neither being present it is reticent,

confining itself to lust, the way two waves

confronting each other achieve neither turbulence

nor passivity. The specificity invoking action

must be isolated through perception

and assigned being and function.

Thus darkness is associated with black

and with presence, not absence. Its function

is that of hiding. It is the vehicle of intoxication,

sleep or violence. And it is in these

that we seek, if not redemption, at least satiation.

It has coalesced into a shape
Recall how your anger
And your scalp heaves.
Saccharine as any death,
As obviously as a woman.
The highway invariably curves
And is associated with wind.
Everything.
Is sufficient to record
Of air. Your lips sing
You find yourself
Constantly. You are questioning
Of beaches. You are seeking
You into whatever
A new country, or a new sky,
And you sail believing

reminiscent of your face.
obliterates your eyes
You hold your own hands,
and it eyes you
Here you must now decide:
over the earth
You must assume
The distance between your knuckles
the passage
inexorably of baited fish.
approaching you
the existence
a landing which will launch
your palms foretell:
pink as any lips,
stars do not move.

It is an asymmetrical sympathy which allows for this confusion:
The emotion which stands as a twin beside the object always
refracts the image causing it to appear to grow or rest
obliquely as if it were partially uprooted by wind, dangerous
and slowly dying.

The land lulls and consumes.
And confuses us with its brittle rhymes.
The fantastic hunt perpetuated
Will lead us back
Permitted to delineate space.
There is a single crow perched
Centered exactly between nowhere
Is that of a man suffocating.
And sleep,
To believe its rage is equal
And we leave it

The relentless voice assails
We have hope
by this belief
to the spare vegetation
But invariably
upon a telephone pole
and its voice
It suggests night
but we are not allowed
to our belief in flight,
and the air to themselves.

And the act of leaving is similar
to the way rain distorts the precise perimeters
of dried blood on pavement: that is, dissolution.
Memory is also qualified;
the crime is not erased, but it assumes a position
more distant, as if one were looking
at an undefined object which, though inanimate,
appears to shiver.

It is this movement of leaving which allows progression:
the leaving allows for no immediate goal,
yet somewhere is reached without volition;
thus in flight one arrives at a mountain
where vision is unobstructed and a sense
of safety is pervasive. Still, the existence of rain
does not deny the prior existence of blood
and the rage perhaps sleeps, but its identity
is the twin to the act of suffocation.

We question the young, broken
                              in their desire
for nonduration.
The drift has receded.
Soon the mountains will yellow
                              with distaste,
A quirk which distorts
                              perception.
We have raged against the wall
until it moaned
Through our mouths and still
the geese
Persevere contented
in the knowledge of arrival.
The sky is abstract, a faith
                              undisturbed by sin
And the meadows,
where we stumble, heave
In sympathy. A girl sings
out the window, unaware
The wind sails her breath
                              into our nostrils,
Or that the bland traffic
has made her mute. She waves
To nothing
                              but air.

As if waking into discomfort, it has become the season
of dispersal. The growth of shadows
is evident and is no longer associated with shade,
but with the notion of obliquity and absence
of other growth, though frigidity will grow.
Dying now is interpreted as fruition
and the failure of resurrection is a fear
we must carry into the increasing darkness.
We will pray and horde against its continuance;
we will pray against, and to, a sky
which is purely abstract in the belief
that divine sympathy will be moved to touch tenderly.

In a single movement
Stutters away from us.
Flags announcing the departure
We have found the landscape
As our recollections
Until our homes are as distant
We have confused access
And are invariably awed
A presence informed
The dream of water we long for
Of sorting sand.
And behind succession stands
Our dream, yet we proceed

the space we would consume
Our skin flutters like torn
of our encumbrances.
as distorted and precious
and we have forgotten
as this air.
with our own presence
that the sky remains
by our fantasies:
after bitter nights
Behind stands succession
a wall of water,
our mouths empty.

We have discovered that certain qualities
of light bruise our emotional structure
causing us to see fog as retribution.
This prevents us from action beyond observation.
Thus we confuse what is merely access
with our personal presence, coming to believe
in indivisibility. A succession of selves
is perceived to occupy the universe;
a reproduction beyond the mere formation
through twinning and this, like a circle of mirrors,
is empty and sterile wherein even the act
of dying becomes incestuous.

You assign yourself complacency
To beyond the limits of your voice,
To see violet bent through pine
To breathe or wait for the soil
With death as superficial
Beats its breath
For winter to stand
To pain.
Of the world and you will know
And will return to whatever it was
And not one cloud

as space you reach
real or imagined,
and you are free
to become fecundant
as your pores. The air
against your unending desire
a pane of ice disposed
Your fingers will examine the things
nothing from the touch
that you were not
will have fallen.

To console the soul of the man killed

in unintentional flight. To console the emotions

which remain reeking. To console the rage

of that yard of land nurtured on terror.

What flocks to what consoling? Those areas

that appear as absence in the sky

seek destination without consolation,

and without passion. What we interpret as anger

is sorrow and consoles nothing when the only

viable action is movement. What is important

is that it not remain solely internalized;

there must be an object to place

there on that yard of terror

to absorb all of what appears as absence

in the sky and to console what movement

has flown into stasis.

We know the reek
With wine and stupidity.
To have died for
And the women are as robust
And where breath quivers like dying fish
To desert and seek what air
By the words of those who perfect
Through recitations
And where the flesh is anonymous,
To vanquish from one's feet
That flesh and blinds the eyes
Of its own clarity.
Will be rebuked
Even what grotesque memory
Of repentance is suffocation
Is oblique

where the lips sing fat
It is not worth
or to live for,
as hogs and as bright.
is the place
is not fouled
their failure
before mirrors.
in snow, is the place
an earth that flavors
merely from fear
We are afraid that our faces
and that our words will contort
we may lie, but this rain
and even the light
causing the young to grow distorted

An appropriate intoxication predicates
the capable depth of falling into night
and thus one is freed from decision or guilt.
Reek cannot be divorced from sinning; metabolism
maintains fusion, and silence becomes the symbol
of death and depression. Noise is a barrier
against falling and against self. Identity
is achieved through anonymity with the attendant
intoxication mimicking union. Now you may sing
and dance in a light which is itself intoxicated,
existing cloudily and obliquely like your body
which, while not yet falling, tips in a display
of light-dynamic, seeking the path of least resistance,
and the source of such great clarity.

Not as earth we caress this grief
Or extinguished stars.
We remind ourselves,
And this is not notable
Is pretty and the flavor
Washed onto this beach laying
Bleached with salt
The sea birds are always as loud
Of the future
It is always the same day regardless
In time and their diving
Like our singing does our hope.
Of this folly
Would be to forsake
And its thousand crabs clinging
Would burst or, at least,
Of some other,
The way shot animals roll
Dreamily at whatever fear
Through, like a jetty or a forest
From inside.
Then that fragrance
Will surround us.

but as dregs
Being futile,
every era is horror
but the dressing
passive as any fish
as we have thrown our bodies
and contentedly reeking.
as the promise
which never arrives, here
of where it falls
makes the air ragged
The place is the vehicle
and to move the body
the pier shuddering
until the tides
arrive in the disguise
more palatable, terror
their eyes
they have just passed
or a night made dark
And if we move toward it
which the smoke surrounds

Each paralleling and being

the other, it is crucial, though impossible,

to differentiate. The imagined white

slab stones juxtaposed are lust,

are metaphysics, and your real

failure is reluctance, perhaps denial,

of identity. All are twins; all twins seek

the enemy, the monster, themselves.

It is in the meandering, in the killing,

the touching that stars cease to define space.

You may dismiss the ocean as symbol;

the imageless shall prevail:

there can be no surrounding and no fragrance.

This dreary symphony,
The wind pursuing itself in fits.
Enough to be believed,
Of soot? Or must we consume
Announces with humility?
Against sleet, merely what is heralded
Will sing. We have burdered
A hundred times and still
Into another.
For perhaps a week
Into some undifferentiated

premeditated display of leaves,
Have we faltered
that the sky is a table
what dregs the season
There is no resonance
as sleep
this road north
it mutates
The magpie remains motionless
but is inevitably transformed
absence.

In the absence of wind one must console onself
to the trajectory of failure which, being inevitable,
has the same rhythm as several doors slamming
in dissonance. Such cacophony is symbol
and is true, disavowing the beauty we believe inherent
in love and pain. Instead, there is the distance of lacking:
believing in the apparent presence
and choosing to accept the apparent.

To have found the labors. The have is. To dissipate.
Intoxication is: thus is rubble. The voice participates
in its own silence: to attempt opacity. The symbolism
refuses universality; yet reaches. Likewise, the gesture
of sunflowers. Ignorance is not excuse; we speak
of inclination and perhaps declination.

Which flaunts the gray, pointless bearing,
Reticent as history.
Blown off through whatever air
Words: enigmatic ice-floes
There are fish frozen
Fugitives who will assuredly awaken.
Wine is obsolete.
Of the body of fear. To touch
Is to touch the sky.
Perhaps we can roll the landscape up
A thief, with the garment
Corner of our past
Of some woman
Will no longer be
Madly and no one

a ship
Quibble with the feathers
has never been breathed.
in spring.
beneath our skates,
No?
Beer is sleep, a violation
the body of a women
And to touch the sky?
and depart,
and hide it in some lost
where we will touch the body
and revel in sky. Then our hands
a part of us. Our lips will sing
will believe us.

Weather, whatever—because the soul is undefined—assaults.
Not truely being suicidal, or understanding, but intrigued,
weather becomes theatrical, like crying at jokes.
Personification of winter is difficult because there is no
character one can project with sincerity. Thus we wither.
Whether it will spring is psychotic fear,
but the question is available and must be addressed
even if memory is the only basis for hope. Snow
is tangible. To kill oneself in snow seems plausible
in exactly the manner in which ice bobs,
without pretension, or person, in a river.

Brilliant light attests
Float by recklessly.
Into the wash. We would taste
Bury ourselves to be resurrected
The landscape is strewn
Of our failure.
In the last laughter
Snow heaves toward us
The sky reels.
Smiling, remembering
And thin as brush smoke
Blowing south

to our dissent. The seasons
Blossoms have fallen
the land with fullness,
with knowledge.
with relics
A black widow ruminates
of the beer can.
as benevolent as stone;
We awaken in the borrow-pit,
we dreamt we could fly.
we hear the voices of geese
along the blue mountains.

The violence with which smoke strikes
the ground repudiates the manner in which geese
seem to float through their voices; and the existence
of blue is a distortion created by distance.
This is not to dismiss the romantic texture
fall pronounces through the air,
but the dream of flight. It is not merely snow,
but the pace that heaves, and one glides
away from oneself with a violence
that can only be contained within despair.

The sparking weeds are not stars,
yet one believes they could touch,
and coldness be tempered by one.

Autumnal disbelief:
The falling snow,
We receive the gifts of discontent,
Giving the word as if it were the lips.
Bucking through waves
And it is the momentum
Tabulating this disbelief
To explain nothing
The purpose is to paint,
The wooden darkness
With the cruel weight of beauty.
This suffering
From the innate fallacy:
Pigeons fall in flames, the time-piece
By dirt,
Where the heart resides

We have attempted to see
but are blinded. Now
of prejudgement:
There is a boat
of snow
we must recall. We are
with symbols
to ourselves again.
like fireflies,
that seems to breathe
We have followed
and still we are not rescued
the violin plays the bones,
is destroyed
and commonplace: beside the place
Is interminable darkness.

Thinness of voice is the distinction
between arrival and departure and is not a song
of love but reiteration of unity:
that in transition is a concrete sky, a path
distinguished only by direction.

There is no number which corresponds
to evolution through time; the arbitrary
remains exalted because the naming process
fails to exact permanence.

Perhaps contrary to this is the consumption of dirt.

Yet both are subsumed under reverential process.

We bleed for what we have bled
Is tenacious, impossible,
Rises off the river ice, collapses
For continuity. It is the same
Of vacuity: white.
Standing on the frozen river, a prayer
Impeccable leaves,
Is brittle against the skin
Sufficient. There is no odor,
Possibly that of collapse.
Is white and that our presence
Duration in such.

the landscape
a resplendent skin. Smoke
into itself, a battle
as our names: a kind
It is a presence to itself,
with leaves,
in our hands. The sky
of our foreheads. This is
possibly no sound,
What is certain is that air
exists for a short

Defeat is finally acknowledged,

in the nature of gravity, the way snow slides away

from ascent and revelation.

Like gravity, and betrayal of ascension,

there is the confrontation of movement:

this is what finally kills; there is no inaccessibility

to either height or revelation.

The woman is in a posture portraying beauty,

call it repose; and the sublime becomes submersion.

This is acknowledged much in the way that dreaming

is accepted: this is defeat; this is ascension.

The way birds arise from the hand,

this is defeat in the manner of speech;

more precisely in the manner of returning.

And to defeat is return, the posture of settling.

Always God's lonely wind
And yet we would suggest
Accompanied by this music
Or non-spiritual pain.
Be it chaos, or vomiting
And the line must extend vertically
Then there will be rest
Of blood on the ground
There, it feeds nothing
Its presence is unexceptional.
Or intelligence involved,
And nothing symbolic:
Lava piled up to prevent
What must remain sustained.
Across pavement

breaks the black walls
nothing arrives
which connotes blood
It must be fenced,
drunks or dogs,
even beyond blue.
or the tranquillity
flowing into our blood.
decisively or particularly,
There is no telepathy
merely perception;
The black walls are only broken
what is not wanted from entering
The rattle of a leaf
is that.

Absence of sentiment is considered failure
and requires apology. The faceless
is considered coincidental
to the presence of cliffs. Death here is easy,
in fact lustful, and what ensues is merely purgation.
This is inevitable and requires no apology.
Sacrificial death, of whatever
sentiment, is deemed sacrosanct,
even if the digging is muddy and darkness
is the inevitable vehicle.
Yet daylight exists and the space
one must occupy is seething with an illumination
in which one is forced to find the distance
between one's fingers unbearable.

An edifice which is eternal,
Portrayal of dirt,
Tree in juxtaposition
Of clouds defining
The reward for your patience
Will not console harvest
Children will consider
To intoxication. Music
In autumn leaves. The profound
Is edifice, is opaque. Character
To sunlight and air. The distance
Is a grid dependent
Descends. Your contemplation
The appearance of particularities
And is fallacy. Perhaps the solution
Edifice, dirt. Or perhaps it begs.
Not confront your body violently,
Though will demand of your leisure
For the accomplishment of edifice
And that, surviving,
You hope, as the entrance
And the exit.

not your lips'
but dirt. Consider one
to your death or the affectation
the perimeter and your gestures.
will be food and denial. Rain
nor your repetitive births.
the past deleterious
shall not be compared to wind
systemization of notions
can be reduced
between fences
on the angle at which vapor
of time presumes
in specific spaces
will be love, not
Regardless, you will
nor your sentiment,
pain,
or facade for pain.
will justify the rest,
subsumes the icy gate

Having been resurrected from your imagination,
or threat of death, you arrive to find yourself
as you were: trying to immortalize what you imagine.
This is essential, not just as distraction,
or spiritual blindness, but as method;
and the method is essential for moving yourself
through time. Otherwise, there would only be stasis
and despair. It is as if one had fabricated
an edifice which is eternal; one wherein each element
is the embodiment of idea. This is not the construct
of language but imposition upon space.
Then what is occupied becomes, in a symbolized way,
spirit and its duration does not bring satiation,
but lust for further occupancy
and the possibility of a sleep which is entered
with the conviction of arisal.

They continually replay the distinction,
Assert that the cacophony of chairs
Forest or where the separation
Is honest. The vibratory chord
Beneath the hair
Of non-dissipated presence
They believe that in the attendance
Is a continuity, not unlike seasons,
The little cries of distress
And supersedes
Of the dead in the presence
Contrived. Still,
Junctures in the tragedy
That they are amusing themselves
They assume that this act
Beyond the mere creation
The profundity or emotion adequate
There is no intent.
Yet the resonance remains
Worn as a necklace
Of the universe

but cannot
is not Platonically
of blue to green
is exhalted;
the skull hums a lyric
opposed to ash.
of buildings
which preserves
and ecstasy,
the mere piling up
of nothing
they are crying at the wrong
and are unwilling to concede
for the duration.
carries a significance
of vibration which has not
to affect change.
There is no causality.
like a tuning fork
to collect the dissonance
and direct it into the heart.

Danger, in this environment, is sexual,
a way of interpreting the articulation
of a wrist or lip.

Speech is a costume wherein intention
is disturbed by the reflected light from a window
forcing the impression of sincerity.

To dismiss the illusion one must discern
the space between the antagonist's eyes;
therein lies arbitrary fallacy.

This is related to archetypes in that violent
gestures are self-conscious: the manner
in which actors bend.

And danger, in environment, is sexual,
a way of succeeding by imposition; a stance
which, though barren, calls.

To this, what hand remains, moves, slightly,
skyward, earthward.

It is all notions which we,
Have accepted as the basis
In the manner in which we do.
Not only themselves, but the fearful
The sky unto itself.
Become terror;
As sublime; its palate as genuine.
Is sobbing at the thought
Of that which is essentially artifice:
Of the damned;
The fear is that it will slip
And we will be faced with the face
To obscurity: God's
That which is designed
Of sand by wind or some other
To which we have failed to bow.

in some delirium,
for living
The words betray,
hope which balances
Its modulations
its noise is identified
Yet the man
of the extinction
the instruction
the edification of the condemned.
out of possession
we have relegated
our own, or more likely
around the movement
mundane presence

One observes, as in palmistry, or a fired tortoise shell,

the cracking floor and in randomness of pattern assumes

that there is a presence, if not divine, at least greater

than doubt. The hands are not required to mirror this,

actually or gesturally, yet the continuity of principle

remains observed.

There is no attendant image.
The process has been without
Gray bark exudes not
Of the sound evolves
There is nothing
In presence:
Does not establish itself.
Is to act some compelling response:
Slovenly with meaning
Or other exquisite failure.

From inception
body. Ragged
even fragrance. The end
as a slap and adrenalin.
convincing or deniable
the contrite voice
Yet the ubiquitous desire
a dance
a disarming glance

"The loon is failure of will.
And sing even though. The gait
Call and touch of moisture.
Your skin,
The dawn a lyric of love.
Is the sum.
Undefinable terror.":

Swim and fall
is a siren
The modulations amend
your brilliant tongue. Sang
Less the cost of drowning
Mation of it roaring at you
Attending.

There is no attendant image. From inception we have waited
with less reluctance. There appears to be a texture
derived from our inappropriate postures: swan or snake.

There is no attendant fragrance. From inception
we have been devoid of personality, humoring ourselves
with gestures inappropriate to the texture
of our voices which, like music, repudiate the odors of women.

There is no attending. The occupancy of space is sufficient
to sustain the humor eternally or, if not, briefly.

`The day is insurgent
From falling stars
Omniscience. We are satisfied
On the cane;
To soil/desire. Yet,
In its brilliance,
The pious morbidity
In the very artifacts
With passive groans

Bemoaned, yet loved,
To rectify chaos/falling star;
What death and time have removed;
Our random designs
In the stasis of indifference:
Whole. And we are satisfied:
Float before us, round
Of the sky bedecked
Or falling.

energy, relief
which confuse mythic
with the bud
the mythic is incredulously redeemed
there is a grand hilarity
a clarity which sacrifices
impregnated
for which we lust
and tears.

we give of our day energy
to replace
to imprint
on a landscape immured
through this we become
our full bellies
like the dome
with stars, static

As if within us elation were announced like a performance
we would savor third-hand: this is exactly the manner in which we
greet the day and our over-conscious selves. We consider what
we love in response to the movement of the sun, the way
a child tilts its head toward a passing bird, not merely
in observation and curiosity, but in memory and perhaps
speech. Bemoaned, yet loved, is the legacy of such a posture,
perhaps in memory of a mythic sky—we would hope—or more
likely in the memory of a unit of air we were unable to
transform into something more like ourselves. We assimilate
this failure into ourselves and live, doomed by all means,
in dissonance and pain having discovered that we were static
or falling or, reluctantly, receding away from ourselves
and our image of the world, in the same way that a clock
is turned back at a certain time to provide more light
at another time.

The falling day is involate,
Determined by our height.
Like a slow meditation
And insects are beyond address.
With alert faith
Is fragrant with ignorance
It is not merely the dog
That give clarity
And the eyes.
For tools
And still possess them
The most impossible
And our name becomes extant,
Than our arms.
The silent plane
Assumes an unprecedent distance
Then clouds become clouds.

its duration
Summer wears
where designs of stalks
We caress the hour
and that hour
allowing us to live.
or the pigeons
and depth, but the light
It is then our hands grope
which they are unable to comprehend
with certainty.
and joyous twist our lips
a presence greater
Then our voice grids
and the landscape
and familiarity.

Being twins we have no memory and perceive ourselves
as statues which, while volatile, are recumbent.
In defiance we name ourselves cloud, or water,
and desire permanence.

Intending grandeur, expecting perfection,
we are confronted with an object-in-motion
which fails to satiate. There is no sense of futility,
only perplexity, accentuated with the expression
of one who discovers that, apparently, their eyes
have ceased to be blue.

Holding ourselves, we hold ourselves,
and imagine this emotion to be an edifice,
perhaps a wall or moat which, though tangible,
is invisible to those we do not love.

The oppressive
Sadness in granite and lake,
Symbols or divine.
Refuse of emotion:
Nailed to a tree.
How many articulated waves?
What one has seen, forever?
Is redundancy,
Stone
Stone
Stone
Stone
Stone
Stone
Stone

memory, music, embeds
lyric. These cannot be
What transpires becomes
wooden doll
How many steps?
Must one, incredulously, see
Sleep
unmitigated refrain:

Distance and cold are perceived as facets of despair,
so duration and sensation are rejected as vehicles of pleasure.

The leaves fall all at once, not as cascade, but deflation.
This is more than an image of sorrow; it is distance and cold.

You are alone at this point and are confronted by each stone,
each patch of snow; each unequivocally is duration, sensation.

You are afraid now and are confronted by each object of memory
which you seek to melt or break or cause to fall away.

You are cold and are moving hesitantly in the manner
of a shadow which seems to possess snow.

Emotion survives itself   not through duration
Of rage   but by attachment
To an attendant image.   There is austerity
Even in the garish,   like a flowered
Roadside cross.   Yet the image must not become emotion:
There can be no lust   of street, pathos
Of tree. Sky cannot be despair.

Yet this is both negation and affirmation: affirmed: Sky;
Negated: despair/sky.   The suicidal symbolically abandon
Their hands   knowing that it is these
With which they touch.   Still, soil does not contrive
To be them   or their emotion.

The symbol for struggle: the odor of burning hair.

The movement is an edifice of error

wherein every direction is confused

and the pointing hand is merely desire.

The objects of both desire and familiarity

assume a distance and an aura of distaste,

the way you wake into night

nauseous with the odor of burning hair.

You would like to rescue yourself

but you are obsessed with symbols.

The nights are personified   by odors, a stance
Which deliberately destroys the name.   Torn flesh
Is the brand of edifice   and is soothed
By a night of water.   Must we, in the undifferentiated,
Speak and thus break the odor   down to a color
Or musical note?   Is the night of water
Also C-sharp or blue?   Still, this is confusion:
What we seek to possess as object   is unnamed
Desire. There can be no name.   We call desire
By animal or motion.

The odors are personified   by nights, where we split
tangible air   as if it were the body
Of an animal   we wear as a disguise.
Then we could be the night   of carp and desire
The odor of water;   we could be a wind
Whitening water   or the sound of wings.
None of which will help: the desire to be all
Moves us to name ourselves new;   to cloak ourselves
In a sound or color or odor   and have what is mortal
Within us left to night.

Having come to decide in favor of forgetting,
the fixtures are altered in the room
to give the impression of growth and change.
Yet there are marks in the air
where someone has spoken, perhaps with violence,
which are not merely resonance, but capable of being
more than recalled. This leads to fear
and the sensation of being observed,
like squinting in pretense at night at
someone who has turned their back
away from whatever glare may have seeped in.

What gate posits transcendence:
within which one stands,
Trees, wind? There is no impetus
Brilliance is recumbent
The stream, never ice.

                        the shadow
            the odor which is inclusive,
                    toward motion;
                in effortless arrival;

            Within which one stands, the gate
                and the world buttressed
                  the absorbed is image

Which is to lean
For wind and seeing. No motion,
Or the residue of motion.

            The gate is shadow and does not touch
What air would move it for action.   Falling can be leaf
Or night. And there is no satisfaction   in doing
Or undoing: the gate will be fallen.

The sky landscape is an emotional structure
which determines the degree of our distaste
or elation. To wake under despair
is commonplace; to sleep beneath intoxication
is brilliant. Yet this geography
attempts the delineation of the future
as if it were possible to transgress aware;
as if there were prescribed moments
of emotional identity, like shrines,
where one could know something beyond
brief duration. Still, this landscape
represents only deceit
and one discovers the gesture
with which virga falls is identical
to the soft movement of wind
where nothing grows.

———————————————